AWUMPALEMA

A TRADITIONAL TALE FROM AFRICA

Long ago, in Africa, there was a time when no rain fell. No grass grew, either, and the animals were hungry and thirsty.

But they all knew that there was a magic tree in the forest. They knew that if any animal called out the name of the tree, food would drop from the branches.

The problem was that none of the animals knew its name!

The hungry animals gathered around King Lion.

"What can we do?" they asked.

"I have heard that the mountain spirit knows the name of the magic tree," said King Lion. "Let us send someone to find out."

"Yes, yes!" cried the animals. "But who will go?"

"I am the fastest runner," replied Cheetah. "*I* will go!"

So Cheetah set off. She raced up to the top of the mountain.

Then Cheetah bowed low. "Mountain Spirit," she said, "we are hungry and thirsty. Please tell me the name of the magic tree that will feed us."

"Its name is Awumpalema. Do not forget it!" replied the mountain spirit.

Cheetah raced back down the mountain.

"I am so fast that I won't have *time* to forget it!" she thought. But just then she ran into a huge anthill.

CRASH! Ears over tail she went.

Cheetah limped back into the forest.

"Quick, what is the name?"
cried the other animals.

"It's Awum ... Awum ... Awum ...
Oh, I have forgotten," gasped Cheetah.

The hungry animals were disappointed. They held another meeting to decide who was to go and discover the name of the magic tree.

"I have the best memory," said Elephant. "*I* will go!"

So Elephant set off.

He lumbered up to the top of the mountain.

"Mountain Spirit," he trumpeted, "Cheetah has forgotten the name of the magic tree. Tell me, and I will remember."

"The name of the magic tree is Awumpalema. Do not forget it!" replied the mountain spirit.

Elephant set off down the mountain. "An elephant *never* forgets," he thought.

But just then a little mouse popped out and ran in front of him. Elephant hated mice. He raced back to the forest, his trunk flying.

When he got there, he had forgotten the name of the magic tree!

The other animals were disappointed.

"We are so hungry!" they cried. "Who *can* we trust to bring back the name?"

Tortoise had not spoken before, but now she said, "I will bring back the name of the tree."

The other animals didn't believe her. "You are too small and too slow," they laughed. But Tortoise was determined.

Tortoise began her long, slow journey. On she trudged, all day and all evening, up to the top of the mountain.

"Great Mountain Spirit," she said humbly, "Cheetah and Elephant have both failed. Will you tell *me* the name of the magic tree?"

This time, the mountain spirit replied: "Listen carefully, for this is the last time that I will tell anyone. The name of the magic tree is Awumpalema. Do not forget it!"

Tortoise thanked the mountain spirit and plodded back down the mountain.

"Awumpalema," she thought to herself as she passed the mouse.

"Awumpalema," she thought to herself as she passed the anthill.

"Awumpalema," she thought to herself as she came to the edge of the forest.

Finally, she came to where the other animals waited around the magic tree.

"Awumpalema!" shouted Tortoise, and delicious food of all kinds began to drop from the tree. Water welled up from its roots to make a deep pool. All the animals began to eat and drink.

And from that time on, no one ever laughed at Tortoise for her slowness.

ACKNOWLEDGEMENTS

We are grateful for the advice and suggestions of the following people: Tod Boley, Ron Chase, Jerome Lawson, Carmen Massey, Mark Peppard, and Paul Rosenthal.

NOTE

Doubtless, in your wandering through the mesas and arroyos of TV's horse opera country, you have heard the term "homestead" used to describe certain land laws of the United States allowing settlers to obtain free federal land. This book has absolutely nothing to do with these laws. If your primary interest is in raising a few chickens or perhaps a pig or two on a place of your own, the best advice we can give is to put down this book and go get a *Whole Earth Catalogue*. But if you are interested in protecting that place of your own so you can raise your chickens with peace of mind, then this book can be of great value.

1
HOW TO USE THIS BOOK

2
HOMESTEAD PROTECTION: AN OVERVIEW

A. How a Declaration of Homestead Works 2/1
    1. Forced Sales
    2. Voluntary Sales

B. What Kinds of Homes Are Protected 2/6

C. Declared and 'Automatic' Homesteads 2/6
    1. Boats, Motor Homes and Other Dwellings
    2. Selling Your Home Voluntarily
    3. Forced Sales

D. How Much Equity Is Protected 2/9
    1. Single Owners: $30,000
    2. Family Units: $45,000
    3. Disabled, Older or Low-Income Owners: $75,000
    4. If Your Status Changes

E. Who Needs to Record a Declaration of Homestead 2/14

F. Who Can Record a Declaration of Homestead 2/15

G. When To Record a Declaration of Homestead 2/16

H. Will Declaring a Homestead Hurt Your Credit? 2/17

I. Debts Not Covered by Homestead 2/18
    1. Child Support and Alimony
    2. Mortgage (Deed of Trust) and Home Equity Loans
    3. Taxes

3

HOW TO PREPARE AND FILE A HOMESTEAD DECLARATION

    A. Choosing the Right Form 3/1

    B. Filling Out the Declaration 3/1
        1. Declaration of Homestead (Individual)
        2. Declaration of Homestead (Couple)

    C. Getting the Declaration Notarized 3/7

    D. Recording the Declaration 3/7

4

DEATH, DIVORCE AND BANKRUPTCY

    A. Death 4/1
        1. Death of a Joint Owner
        2. Protection for Surviving Family Members
        3. New Non-Family Member Owners

    B. Divorce 4/4
        1. Separate Property
        2. Community Property

    C. Bankruptcy 4/5